THE BEST ME! BEHAVIOUR

Wailing Won't Work!

by

Kimmie Auntie

Illustrations by

Ayeshe Sadr & Ishaan Dasgupta

another title brought to you from

the **BEST ME** series

SCHOLASTIC

New York Toronto London Auckland

Sydney New Delhi Hong Kong

For my true friend Miek: a stunningly inspiring mom, golden-shine life compass, sassafras incarnate ... and fearless hair dyeist.

Published by Scholastic India Pvt. Ltd.
A subsidiary of Scholastic Inc., New York, 10012 (USA).
Publishers since 1920, with international operations in Canada, Australia, New Zealand, the United Kingdom, India, and Hong Kong.

For information regarding permission, write to:
Scholastic India Pvt. Ltd.
A-27, Ground Floor, Sigma Centre
Infocity-1, Sector 34, Gurgaon 122001 (India)

This edition: October 2022

ISBN-13: 978-93-8610-678-0

Printed in India at Sterling Graphics Pvt. Ltd., Manesar

Dear friend,

The thing is—life is better when you smile.
That's it.

Truly,

Kimmie Auntie

"I want five more toffees!"
Vidya demanded.

Papu replied,
"Vidya, I love you
and I want you to
be healthy—
no more toffees."

So Vidya threw herself on the floor and wailed.
Oh dear.

But Papu still didn't give her more toffees.

The next day, Vidya ordered, "I want to watch TV!"

Dadima answered, "I love you—and too much TV rots your brain!"

And so Vidya kicked, sobbed and wailed.

Oh dear.

But Dadima still sent her outside to play.

The next day, Vidya charged,
"I don't want to go to sleep!"

Mum hugged her. "I love you— and you need sleep to go to school and play tomorrow!"

And so Vidya pouted,
made a stinky face,
threw herself about,
AND wailed.

Oh dear.

But Mum still tucked her in,
kissed her forehead, and
turned out the light.

Vidya was wailing
all of the time!
What were they going to do?

Sargam put on her thinking cap ...
and hatched a Grand Plan.

The next evening, the family sat down to munch popcorn and sign Diwali cards. As Vidya grabbed her shiny magenta pen, she wailed, "I don't want to sign cards! I want to colour."

Oh dear.

But this time, Sargam was ready with her Grand Plan. She smiled, "That's alright, Vidya—I will sign for you."

Papu, Mum, and Sargam signed cards for an hour.
They signed cards for their aunties;
they signed cards for their teachers;
they signed cards for Papu's business.
They signed a LOT of cards.

Then Papu looked over Sargam's shoulder. "Sargam—you are signing your name with a smiley face. But why are you signing Vidya's name with a frowny face?"

Vidya jerked up from colouring,

WHAAT!

Sargam explained, "Well, I am a happy child so I signed mine with a smiley face. But Vidya wails all the time. So I just signed her name with how she looks—a frowny face!"

Papu, Mum and Sargam all looked at Vidya.

Vidya flipped her hair back and thought about wailing ...
But then she WOULD have a frowny face. She didn't
want to be the girl with a frowny face!
What could she do?

Maybe she could turn her frowns ... upside down?

The next day Vidya wanted a toffee.
Instead of wailing, she asked nicely,
"May I have one toffee, please?"

Papu was quite surprised. "Sure—you can have one."
And he handed Vidya her favourite strawberry flavour.
Vidya gave Papu a big smile.

The next day when Vidya wanted to watch TV, she politely spoke, "Can I watch TV now?" Dadima replied, "You've had your TV time already, Vidya—please finish your homework or go outside and play."

Vidya thought about wailing ... after all, she DID want to watch TV. But then she remembered the smiley face ... so she skipped outside to play in the sunshine with her friends.

The next day, she didn't want to go to bed yet. But instead of wailing, she sweetly cooed, "Will you read me a story before bedtime, Mum?"

"Sure, Vidya—I'd be happy to.
But then it's bedtime for sure!"

Vidya smiled. She loves reading stories ...
and so she tucked herself into bed with no wailing.

After her story, Vidya snuggled down in the covers. She whispered to Sargam, "Didi—it is so much nicer to not wail. I get strawberries, sunshine, stories ... and smiles!"

And Sargam hugged her goodnight.

The Grand Plan was a Grand Success!

Discussion Questions for Parents and Teachers:

Why is it important for children to learn that wailing is not the way to get what they want?

How can you make sure your child knows you love them—but loving them does not mean they get anything they want?

Why is it important for adults to help children learn to handle disappointment?

Activities:

1. Have your child draw a picture of a frowny face on a paper plate. Explain to them how they can turn it "upside down" to make the frowny face into a smile!

2. Role play with the children. When they would like something, help them walk through how to ask for it. But they still don't get it every time!

*Parenting Tip: If your child is still struggling with wailing after he has read this book, just ask, "Where's the smiley face?" If need be, ask them to leave the area. Explain the family space is for happy children, and when they are happy they are welcome to come back. But, DO NOT give the child what they want or they will learn in life that wailing is the way to go! (And we all know nothing is worse than a waily adult!)